Nougat

HOW THEY USED TO DO IT

Copyright © 2013 Two Magpies Publishing
An imprint of Read Publishing Ltd
Home Farm, 44 Evesham Road, Cookhill, Alcester,
Warwickshire, B49 5LJ

Commissioning Editor Rose Hewlett
Words by Sophie Berry
Design by Zoë Horn Haywood

All Images remain the copyright property of their respective owners, all attributions and copyright licences are referenced at the rear of the book. This book is copyright and may not be reproduced or copied in any way without the express permission of the publisher in writing.

British Library Cataloguing-in-Publication Data A catalogue record for this book is available from the British Library.

Contents

Foreword	1
Introduction	3
History of Nougat	7
Story of the Store Cupboard	11
Wartime Rationing	19
Sourcing Your Supplies	23
Equipment	27
Measurements	33
~ Cup Conversions	36
Temperature	37
~ The Drop Test	44
Techniques	45

Contents

Recipes	49
~ Brown Nougat Recipes	51
~ Regional White Nougat Recipes	59
~ White Nougat Variations	69
~ Wartime Recipes	81
The Etiquette of Serving	87
Gifts	91

Foreword

'Knowledge never learned in schools'

Watson, 1891

The simple pleasure of mastering practical household skills has been all but forgotten over the last century. We live in an overly convenient, disposable world in which things arrive pre-packed, ready-wrapped and lacking in any craft, care, or quality.

It's time to reject this attrition of what were once everyday skills, time to get back to basics, time to remember How They Used To Do It.

The How They Used To Do It series will take you back to the golden age of practical skills; an age where making and mending, cooking and preserving, brewing and bottling, were all done within the home. The series will instruct you in a whole range of traditional skills that have fallen out of use, putting old knowledge into new hands. Using household items, nifty hints and tricks, and a little creativity you will be surprised what you can achieve.

The series has been carefully curated from a wealth of original resources to provide a wonderful blend of social history and practical instruction. The knowledge within these pages has been sourced from rare books, old newspapers and forgotten magazines to inform a whole new generation about How They Used To Do It.

Introduction

WELCOME TO THE WONDERFUL WORLD OF NOUGAT MAKING.

Introduction

With this little book in your hands, you can turn even a humble kitchen into a hub of nougat-making activity, happily passing many a rainy afternoon creating mouth-watering treats. As well as lots of classic recipes this book is filled with nougat-making tips and techniques you can try as soon as you have mastered the basics.

What's more, you don't need lots of equipment or a vast array of ingredients to get started. Pleasingly, most of the equipment you will need will be found already tucked away in your cupboards and cutlery drawer.

Introduction

The beauty of making your own nougat is that you can be sure to use the best and purest ingredients. In an age which tends to be increasingly synthetic, knowing exactly what has gone into your lovingly created confectionery is surely an attractive prospect.

Added to this, the result of nougat-making at home is often much thriftier than buying it ready made. By only making what you want, and in quantities you need, there is no waste.

History of Nougat

History of Nougat

Nougat is a firm, chewy confection which has been enjoyed as a sweet treat for centuries. It consists of sugar, sometimes honey, nuts and often beaten egg.

Nougat is likely to have originated in southern Europe and it is thought that white nougat first appeared in Italy during the 15th century, and is made with beaten egg whites and honey, among other ingredients.

Other early nougat recipes can be traced back to a region in France, Montélimar, which is

History of Nougat

where the name Montélimar nougat came from. The first almonds trees were introduced to the region in the 17th century by an explorer named Olivier de Serre. Montélimar has since become famous for its nougat and is considered the birthplace of the confectionery.

Another popular type of nougat is called brown nougat, a variant which is sometimes referred to as mandorlato in Italy, or nougatine in French. This kind of nougat is made without the use of egg whites, and so has a firm, crunchy texture.

History of Nougat

Today, a modern variation of nougat is often found as an ingredient in a whole host of modern-day chocolate bars, which differ from traditional recipes. This difference came about due to the rise in the use of corn syrup in the early 1900s which was whipped with eggs and gelatin to produce the very light soft confection. Despite the rise in popularity of this new-style nougat, the traditional classic recipes still remain popular.

Story of the Store Cupboard

Story of the Store Cupboard

Kitchens have come an awfully long way in the past century, as have the supplies stocked in pantries and larders. Before modern conveniences such as fridges and freezers, one of the biggest hurdles housewives had to overcome was the task of preserving, and it was no mean feat! It is hard to imagine a world without the convenience of modern kitchen appliances, and keeping food fresh was a daily challenge.

There are many simple preservation methods that can be carried out in the kitchen, without the use of modern conveniences. Salt can be used to cure meat and fish, and pickling can preserve vegetables. The drying of fruit, herbs and spices is especially useful, and can be used across a wide range of recipes including sweets.

Story of the Store Cupboard

Sugar is a natural preservative meaning it could be used by housewives alongside some clever cooking to preserve a glut of seasonal produce or dear fruits and nuts. Jam, chutney, marmalade and confectionery could be made and stockpiled for the coming months.

Having a well-stocked larder was the mark of a good housewife, and before easy preservation and storage methods became commonplace, nougat would have been a welcome addition to the larder's shelves. The beauty of nougat is that it will keep for a fairly long time and does not need to be refrigerated.

Story of the Store Cupboard

STAPLE INGREDIENTS

Now, let's take a little time to get to know the ingredients you will need to make nougat at home. You'll be very familiar with most of the ingredients listed in this book, but there may be things that are new to you if you've not made nougat at home before.

Much like with your kitchen equipment, making sure you have the right supplies is very important before you get started. Here are a few pantry staples, with a little explanation:

Story of the Store Cupboard

Sugar

Sugar is a staple ingredient, and these days, it is available in many forms. Ready-to-use sugar is a luxury which we now may take for granted, but using sugar in a recipe used to be a much more laborious process. Until the late nineteenth century, sugar came in the form of sugarloaf. Granulated and cubed sugar came a little later so for a long while, if you wanted to use sugar you had to get to grips with a large sugarloaf cone.

Housewives would buy their sugar in tall, conical loaves, and trim off what they needed with special iron sugar-cutters called sugar nips. If a recipe called for fine, granulated sugar, then a little elbow grease and a pestle and mortar would be enthusiastically employed!

Story of the Store Cupboard

Almonds

Almonds are key to making nougat, and the distinctive flavour is present in many traditional recipes. Almonds have been a key ingredient in sweets since the very earliest confections of the middle ages. Blended with honey, and sticky fruits such as dates, almonds have been enjoyed for thousands of years. Almonds also have a number of health benefits, and will help keep your hair and skin in good condition. They also contain a great amount of protein and fibre, are are high in monounsaturated fats which will help to keep your heart healthy.

Story of the Store Cupboard

Glucose

Glucose is a type of sugar derived from plants. Conveniently, it is sold in powder form and readily available. Glucose is a very useful addition to your nougat as it decomposes much more easily than regular cane sugar, and will prevent your mixture from crystallising. This is very important, as crystallisation can result in your nougat sweets taking on a grainy, gritty texture.

Glucose is available to buy in supermarkets, or in health food shops. It is well worth sourcing this ingredient as it will crop up in a variety of sweet recipes.

Story of the Store Cupboard

Eggs

Eggs are incredibly versatile, and are key to many a white nougat recipe. Beaten egg whites are imperative to the distinctive chewy texture of white nougat, and help keep the confectionery light in texture. Always use the freshest eggs possible, as they will hold more air after being beaten than less fresh eggs. It is important that you beat your egg whites well, if your recipe calls for it. You must beat the egg whites until they form stiff peaks. A good way to test if your egg whites have had enough air added is to hold the mixing bowl you are beating them in upside down. If the egg whites start slipping down the edges, you need to pick up your whisk again and use a little more elbow grease.

Wartime Rationing

Wartime Rationing

During the 1930s, the country's love affair with sugar came under attack. As World War II air raid sirens sounded throughout Britain's cities, a different war was being fought behind closed doors by the country's army of housewives. Trade routes to the UK were targeted during the war, and food supplies quickly dwindled. On 8 January 1940, bacon, butter and sugar were rationed by the government, followed in subsequent months by meat, tea, jam and much more.

Despite being armed with her government-issued ration book containing coupons for all rationed items, the average housewife's weekly shopping basket was suddenly much

Wartime Rationing

lighter than before. Creating tasty and nutritious meals for the family became a real challenge for many.

Sugar became a very precious resource, and a thriving black market quickly sprung up as a result of the strict rationing. With legitimate supplies so very low, mothers had to be increasingly inventive in order to supply their children and husbands with sweet treats.

Wartime Rationing

Many recipes for sweet substitutes were circulated during wartime Britain, with most ingeniously using the natural sugars from fruits and vegetables such as carrots and beetroot. Sweets a real treat, and rationed to 12oz per month, so anything a clever housewife could magic up in the kitchen was seen to be a real coup.

Sourcing Your Supplies

Sourcing Your Supplies

These days, you are lucky that you can make sure your pantry is stocked with all that you might need. Gone are the days of visiting a host of shops to get what you need. Without the convenience of large supermarkets, it could take a busy housewife the best part of the day to fill her shopping basket with supplies for the week from her local high street.

And with such an array of mod cons in the kitchen these days, storing ingredients and preparing sweets has never been easier. With a good selection of nougat-making basics in your store cupboard you can try a huge array

Sourcing Your Supplies

of recipes, without the bother of having to go out shopping every time you want to get a batch of nougat bubbling on the stove.

Finding the best ingredients before you put your apron on and start cooking is important, as the lovelier your ingredients are, the lovelier your nougat sweets will be. Look at the local produce on offer in your area. it is so often the case that the best things to eat are the things that grow locally, are in season, and haven't travelled a huge distance. Not only do these things taste better than their imported counterparts, but it is far kinder to the environment to use what is nearby.

Sourcing Your Supplies

Perhaps you have a wonderful honey producer who can supply you with honey, or a brilliant local health food shop where you can stock up on essences and flavours? Use your local suppliers and their expertise, as their knowledge will be rather useful to you while you are still getting to grips with the basics.

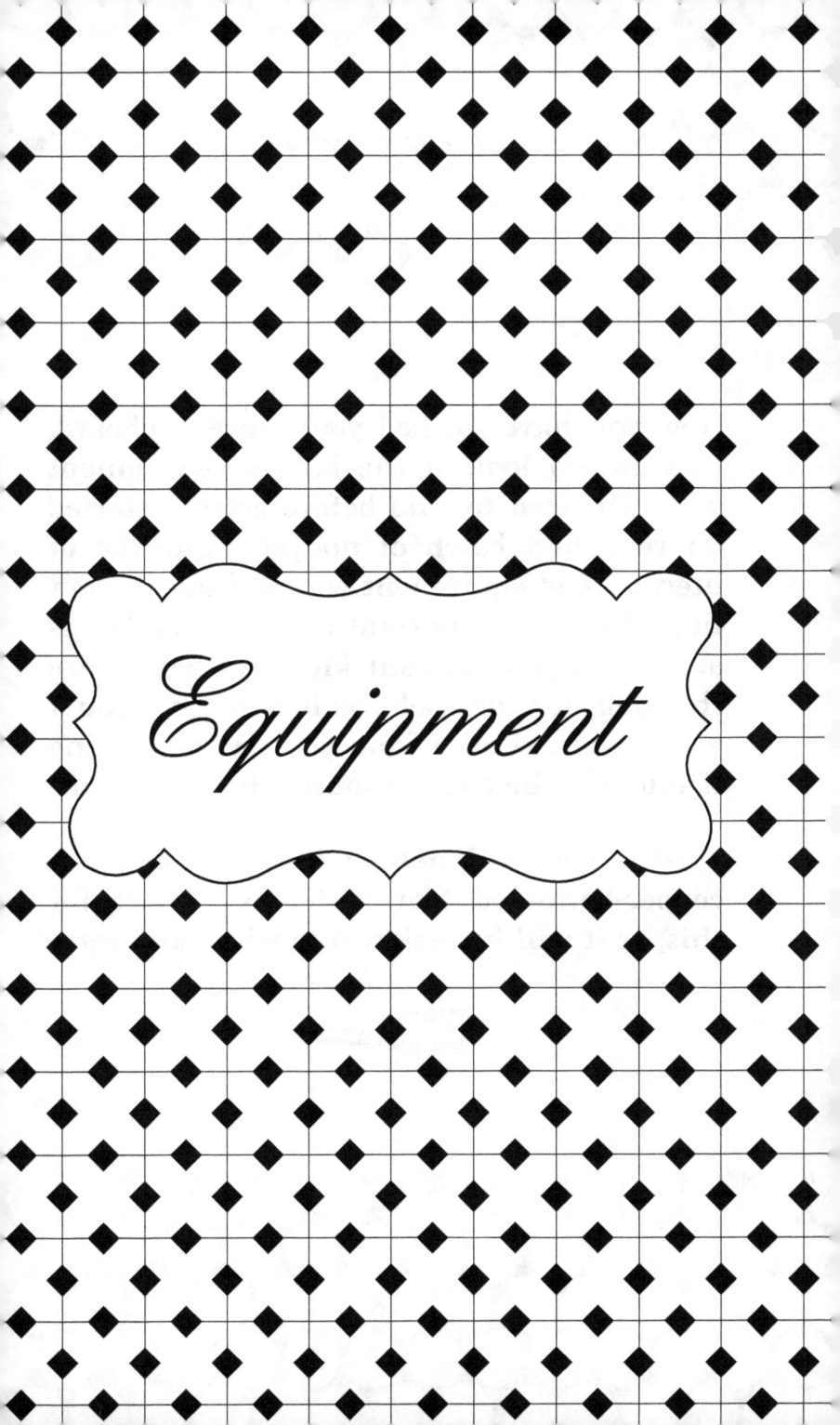
Equipment

Equipment

Now you have stocked your store cupboard, let's have a look at the kitchen equipment you will need to find before getting started on your first batch of nougat . The list of utensils and equipment you will need is not huge, but it is important you have the basics at your fingertips. Your kitchen utensils are the tools of your trade, as it were, and you'll get the best results from your sweet making if you take the time to source the right tools.

Firstly, you will need a large saucepan. A copper-bottomed jam boiler is perfect for this, as it will be designed to withstand very

Equipment

high cooking temperatures, as well as be big enough to contain boiling sugar bubbles. A smaller saucepan will also be necessary, as some recipes require the mixture to be cooked in two batches. A wooden spoon for stirring the mixture is essential, as plastic may not withstand the high temperature of boiling sugar. As well as this, you will also need a spatula or scraper for working your mixture, and a sharp knife to mark your nougat into squares before it cools.

Some recipes call for you to work the cooling mixture, a technique which we explain a

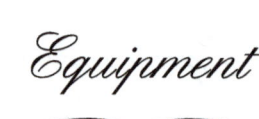

Equipment

little later in this book. A marble slab, or other heatsafe work surface is best for this. Marble would have been the first port of call for kitchen enthusiasts in the early days of nougat making as it stays nice and cool. A portion of old marble wash stand would make the perfect work surface for nougat making, and you can often find these in second hand shops, or at antique fairs.

Equipment

If your nougat recipe does not require working, you will need a large, shallow baking tin to pour your mixture into so it can set. You may also want to invest in some rice paper. Rice paper is a nifty way of wrapping and storing your nougat, and it is also edible. Rice paper is a neat way to finish your carefully prepared nougat sweets.

Equipment

EQUIPMENT CHECKLIST

A LARGE SAUCEPAN
*
A SMALL SAUCEPAN
*
MEASURING CUPS AND SCALES
*
SUGAR THERMOMETER
*
WOODEN SPOON
*
LARGE MIXING BOWL
*
A WHISK
*
BENCH SCRAPER, OR SPATULA
*
SCISSORS OR SHARP KNIFE
*
SHALLOW BAKING TIN
*
RICE PAPER

Measurements

In the most part, measurements in the recipes in this book will be in cups. A small coffee cup is the best kind to use, and make sure you use the same cup to measure all your ingredients.

You may not be familiar with using cups to measure ingredients but they are a quick and easy way of portioning the rather large quantities of sugar,  and other ingredients, some recipes call for.

Cups have been used in cookery for generations, after an American culinary expert called Fanny Farmer introduced them as a standardised form of measurement in recipes. Accuracy and consistency are very

Measurements

important in any recipe, especially for nougat, so Fanny's work was rather groundbreaking at the time.

Fanny published her best-known cookery book 'The Boston Cooking-School Cook Book' in 1896, and it has been used by generations of keen cooks ever since. Fanny introduced these new standardised measurements by stressing the importance of levelling off the cup as you measure. It may seem insignificant, but before her clever intervention, cooks had to make do with instructions such as 'a large dash', 'a goodly pinch', and even 'butter the size of an egg'. Rather amusing, but a little inconsistent, don't you agree?

Measurements

Of course, you don't have to use cups. This table is a handy tool if you need to convert cups into other amounts.

1 cup	8 fluid ounces	½ pint	237 ml
2 cups	16 fluid ounces	1 pint	474 ml
4 cups	32 fluid ounces	1 quart	946 ml
2 pints	32 fluid ounces	1 quart	0.946 l
4 quarts	128 fluid ounces	1 gallon	3.784 l

Temperature

Temperature

Being able to gauge the temperature of your mixture as it cooks is essential when you're making nougat at home. Just a few degrees over or under your desired temperature will result in a very different final product, so it is important that you carefully monitor your nougat mixture as it cooks.

Boiling sugar may seem like quite a demanding task. One must be mindful of safety at all times as it is easy to burn yourself on the cooking mixture. The change in temperature can often be rather rapid so it is very important that you heat the mixture gradually, to avoid a sudden change in temperature.

Temperature

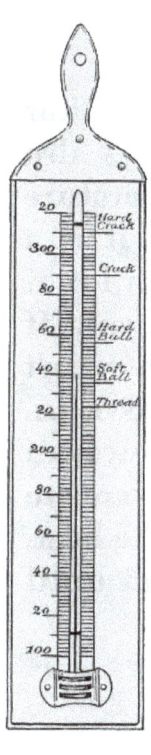

Many of the recipes in this book are classic recipes which have been used in countless kitchens, by generations of cooks. The temperatures stated in the recipes in this book will be in Fahrenheit, as this is the original form of measuring temperature. The metric system which uses the Celsius scale took some time to be introduced internationally, and Fahrenheit is still widely used to this day.

Temperature

A thermometer is the safest way to monitor the temperature of boiling sugar. It is also the easiest way to gauge the exact temperature of your cooking nougat mixture, so it is a good idea to use one until you have a lot of experience working with boiling sugar. If you have a new thermometer which hasn't been used before, make sure you break it in. You can do this by placing it into a saucepan of cold water, and then heating the water to boiling point. Remove the pan from the heat, but leave the thermometer in the pan until the water has cooled.

Temperature

Tip

After use, plunge your thermometer into warm water and wipe with a soft cloth.

Remember to do this rather promptly after you have used it, as the nougat mixture will cool, and be very difficult to clean off later.

Temperature

THE DROP TEST

These days we are lucky that sugar thermometers are readily available and are relatively cheap to buy. This was not always the case. Before the introduction of this nifty household tool, another ingenious method had to be employed to test the temperature of nougat mixture as it cooked.

This age old method is called The Drop Test.

By carefully dropping a little mixture into some cold water, you can gauge the stage the mixture is at by the type of mass the mixture forms. Once mastered, this rather ingenious little skill is a failsafe way of monitoring

Temperature

your nougat mixture, and is a truly authentic confectionery-making method. If you choose to use the drop test method whilst making your nougat, do be mindful of the dangers of boiling sugar. You don't want a nasty burn, so be very careful when testing your mixture.

Most of the recipes in this book will state to heat the mixture to hard ball stage, which is around 250°F to 366°F. If the liquid forms a hard ball when tested in cold water then your mixture has reached the correct temperature.

Have at the table we have provided for more information on regulating the temperature of your nougat mixture without a thermometer. This should give you a good idea of what to look out for at each stage of cooking.

The Drop Test

Stage	Temperature	Uses
Thread - Forms a thin liquid thread	110°C to 112 °C (230 to 234 °F)	Sugar Syrups
Soft ball - Forms a soft flexible ball that can be flattened.	112°C to 116 °C (234 to 241 °F)	Fudge, pralines, fondant and butter creams
Firm ball - Forms a firm ball that will hold its shape but is still malleable	118°C to 120 °C (244 to 248 °F)	Caramel Candies
Hard ball - Forms thick threads from spoon and creates a hard ball that will hold its shape	121 to 130 °C (250 to 266 °F)	Nougat, marshmallows, gummies, and divinity
Soft crack - Forms firm flexible threads	132°C to 143 °C (270 to 289 °F)	salt water taffy
Hard crack - Forms hard brittle threads that snap easily	146°C to 154 °C (295 to 309 °F)	toffee, brittles, hard candy, and lollipops
Clear liquid - Liquid will begin to change colour. Colour ranges from golden brown to amber	160 °C (320 °F)	caramelised sugar, caramel
Brown liquid - Liquid will begin to change colour. Colour ranges from golden brown to amber	170 °C (338 °F)	caramelised sugar, caramel

Techniques

WORKING

Sometimes you will find that a nougat recipe requires you to work the cooling mixture. It is a straightforward technique, and is an effective way to blend colouring and flavouring as well as shape your nougat. Some say that working the mixture by hand gives a wonderfully smooth consistency to your nougat. Once you have mastered this basic technique you'll be able to make an impressive array of nougat at home in your kitchen.

After you take the saucepan of nougat mixture off the heat, leave the mixture to cool for a couple of minutes. Now, it is time to wash your hands, put on an apron, and roll up your

Techniques

sleeves. You'll need a little patience and a spot of elbow grease for this. Wearing a pair of latex gloves will also help protect your hands from the heat.

Once cooled, carefully pour the mixture onto a lightly oiled marble slab or board. A portion of old washstand or work surface is perfect for this, although any heat-safe surface will suffice.

Next, with a bench scraper, begin folding the mixture onto itself repeatedly, working it into the required shape. Keep kneading and folding, especially if you are blending fruit, nut or flavouring into your mixture at this stage. Have a little patience, and repeat this process until the mixture starts to hold its shape.

Techniques

Do bear in mind that working your nougat mixture is not essential. If you wish, you can simply mix your ingredients thoroughly in the pan, before carefully pouring it into the buttered tin. Allow the mixture to set before breaking your nougat into small pieces to serve.

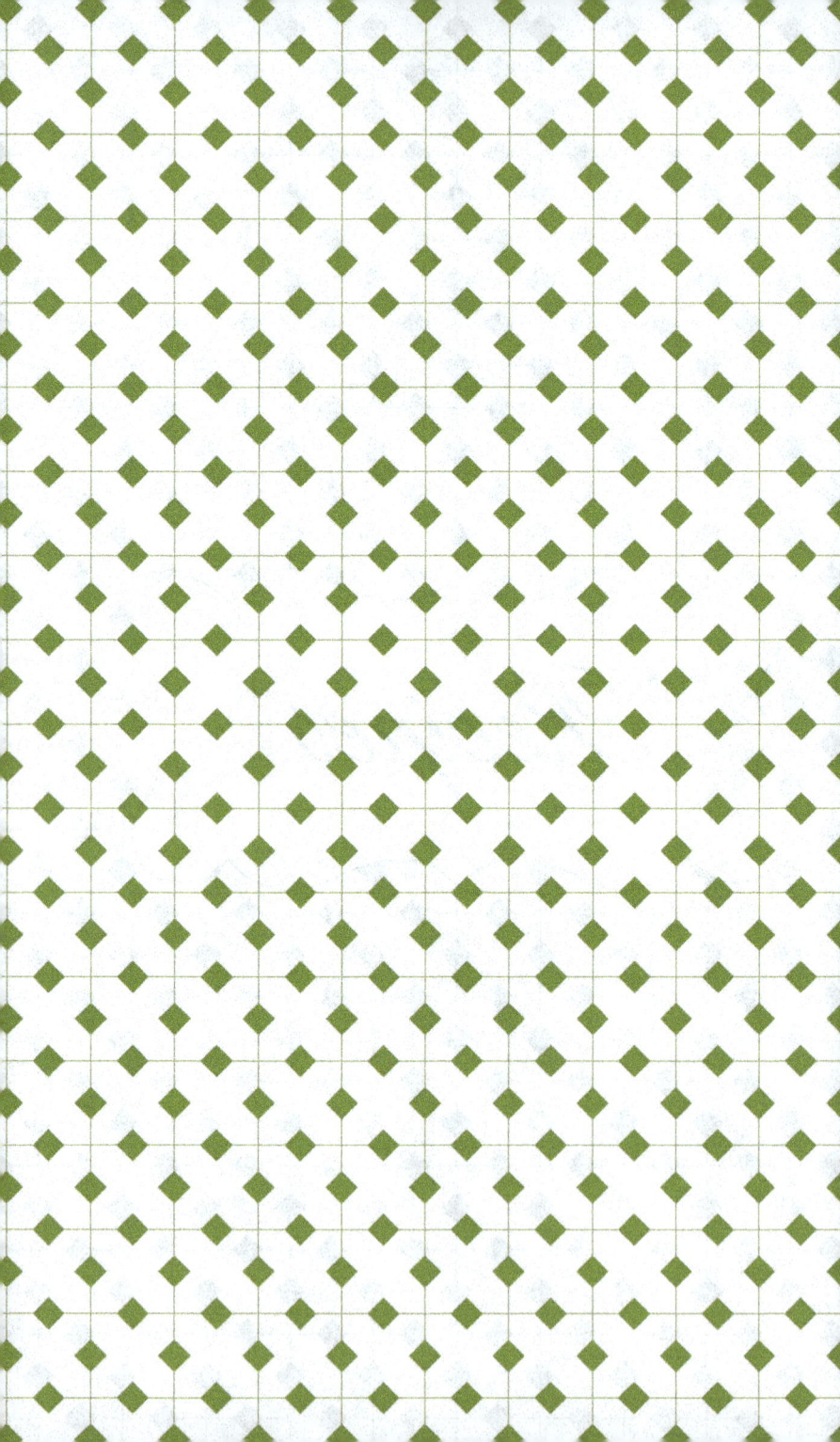

Brown Nougat Recipes

This selection of recipes are for variations of traditional brown nougat, which is made with sugar and nuts, and no egg. Traditionally, almonds form the basis of most classic nougat recipes, but you can use a whole host of other nuts when making nougat. These recipes all use different nuts as a base flavour, from classic almond, to more unusual peanut.

Almond Nougat

Almonds are the classic base of most nougat recipes, and this age-old recipe is still very popular. The almonds give the confection a satisfying crunch while the distinctive flavour of almond is complemented by the sweetness of sugar perfectly.

Almond Nougat

1 lb almonds
1 lb sugar
2 or 3 lemons

1. Blanch the almonds, and carefully split them in half, then quarters. **2.** Spread them over a large dish, and place them in a moderately hot oven - no more than 160°C/320°F, for around half an hour. **3.** In a large saucepan stir the sugar until it has been dissolved by the heat. **4.** Take the almonds out of the oven, and mix with them the juice of the lemons. Put them into the sugar a few at a time, and let them simmer till it becomes a thick stiff paste, stirring it hard all the while. **5.** Have an oiled tin ready and carefully pour your mixture in. **6.** Smooth it evenly, and allow to harden.

Peanut Nougat

Peanuts are more unusual addition to nougat, although perfectly suited to making this confectionery. Peanuts are incredibly high in protein and their nutritional properties have been harnessed and used by cooks and doctors alike for decades.

Peanut Nougat

---

1 lb sugar
3 cups peanuts
¼ tsp salt

---

1. Finely chop the peanuts, and sprinkle with the salt. **2.** In a heavy-bottomed saucepan, stir the sugar over a moderate heat for fifteen minutes, until the sugar becomes a syrup. **3.** Add the nuts, and stir well. **4.** Carefully pour the mixture into an oiled tin, and leave overnight to set. **5.** Cut into squares to serve.

Popcorn Nougat

Popcorn is a much older treat than you may at first expect. Popcorn was first discovered thousands of years ago by the Guatemalans. Popcorn is one of the earliest forms of corn, and has been a popular snack for centuries. The English who came to America in the sixteenth and seventeenth centuries learned about popcorn from the Native Americans, and brought their new-found foodstuff back to Europe.

Popcorn makes wonderful nougat, and is a great way to add different texture to a classic recipe without using nuts.

Popcorn Nougat

2 cups sugar
4 tbsp water
½ tsp lemon extract
1 cup popcorn

1. In a heavy-bottomed saucepan, heat the sugar and water over a moderate heat until the sugar has dissolved. **2.** Add the popcorn, stirring constantly, and cook for a further five minutes. **3.** Remove the saucepan from the heat and add the extracts. **4.** Carefully pour the mixture into an oiled tin, and place in a slightly warm oven until browned. **5.** When cooled, turn out and cut into squares to serve.

Regional White Nougat Recipes

Traditional white nougat recipes have a base of almonds, which are mixed with sugar in much the same way as the brown nougat recipes. The difference lies in the addition of beaten egg white, which gives the final nougat sweets a lighter, more chewy consistency. This next section is dedicated to the many traditional regional variations of white nougat. There are many different versions of the sweet and chewy confection, and here are a few of the best from around the world.

Montélimar Nougat

The first recipe for nougat here for you to try is this classic recipe for Montélimar nougat. The French region was one of the first places where white nougat was made after almonds were first introduced to the Montélimar region by Olivier de Serre, during the eighteenth century. Using the traditional ingredients of honey, egg whites and sugar this recipe creates a wonderfully sweets and chewy confection. The sprinkling of almonds and pistachios also give this classic nougat a lovely crunch.

Montélimar Nougat

3 cups granulated sugar
1 ½ cups honey
¼ cup light corn syrup
1 ½ cups water
6 egg whites
1 tsp lemon zest
2 tsp vanilla extract
1 tsp brandy
2 ½ cups of almonds
⅓ cup chopped pistachios
½ teaspoon salt

1. In a heavy-bottomed saucepan, dissolve the sugar, honey, corn syrup, and water, and bring the mixture to a simmer over medium heat, stirring constantly. **2.** Beat the egg whites while the sugar mixture continues cooking. Beat the egg whites until they form stiff peaks. **3.** Once the sugar syrup reaches 300°F or forms brittle strands when tested in cold water. **4.** Carefully pour the mixture slowly into the egg whites, whisking all the while. **5.** Add the lemon zest and continue whisking the hot nougat mixture for 8 to 12 minutes, until it cools slightly and thickens. **6.** Stir the vanilla, brandy, almonds, pistachios, and salt into the nougat and quickly spread it onto an oiled tin. Gently press down onto the nougat with a spatula so that no air bubbles remain. **7.** Cover the nougat in an airtight container or plastic wrap and allow it to set before cutting and wrapping individual pieces.

French Nougat

Here's another French recipe. Early recipes for nougat are said to have originated from France, and the sweet treat is still enjoyed all over Europe as a traditional Christmas confection. This recipe is slightly more straightforward than the Montélimar nougat recipe, and includes angelica which adds a splash of jewel-like colour to the finished sweets.

French Nougat

1 lb glucose
1 ½ lb sugar
1 cup water
2 egg whites
1 cup blanched and chopped almonds
1 cup candied angelica
1 tsp almond extract

1. First, blanch the almonds and then dry them out in the oven. **2.** In a heavy-bottomed saucepan, boil the glucose, sugar and water until the thermometer reads 270°F, or until the mixture forms a hard ball when tested in cold water. **3.** Beat the egg whites to stiff peaks, and gradually add the syrup, beating all the time. **4.** As soon as the mixture starts to set, add the angelica, almonds, and extract. **5.** Carefully pour the mixture into an oiled tin, and leave to set. **6.** Cut into small pieces when the mixture is set.

Jijona Nougat

Here is a popular Spanish-style recipe for nougat. Nougat is also enjoyed at Christmas time in Spain, and the addition of cinnamon to this recipe makes it a perfect festive treat. It is worth noting that any clear honey will work perfectly well if you cannot find orange blossom honey.

Jijona Nougat

1 cup orange blossom honey
1 cup finely ground almonds
2 egg yolks
1 teaspoon ground cinnamon
½ teaspoon lemon zest
1 egg white, beaten

1. In a heavy-bottomed saucepan, warm the honey over a low heat. Stir in the almonds, and remove the pan from the heat. **2.** Mix the egg yolks, cinnamon, and lemon zest into the almonds. Beat the egg white into stiff peaks and fold into the mixture. **3.** Carefully pour the mixture onto a dish lined with baking paper. Place another sheet of baking paper on top of the mixture and then place a chopping board, or similar on the top to press down on the cooling mixture. **4.** Allow to dry for 3 days. Cut into squares to serve.

Kurtzati-inspired Nougat

The next nougat recipe is inspired by a traditional African type of nougat called Kurtzati. Kurtzati is a white nougat, with the subtle flavour of lemon added. In contrast to classic European versions of nougat, Kurtzati is made with lots of chopped fruits instead of nuts. Sticky fruits like dates and figs work particularly well, but you can get creative and try using any fruit you like.

Kurtzati-inspired Nougat

1 lb glucose
1 ½ lb sugar
1 cup water
2 egg whites
½ cup chopped dates
½ cup chopped figs
1 cup raisins

1. In a heavy-bottomed saucepan, boil the glucose, sugar and water until the thermometer reads 270°F, or until the mixture forms a hard ball when tested in cold water. **2.** In a large bowl, beat the egg whites to stiff peaks. **3.** Gradually add the sugar syrup to the beaten egg whites, beating all the time. **4.** As soon as the mixture starts to set, add the dates, figs and raisins. **5.** Carefully pour the mixture into an oiled tin, and leave to set. **6.** Cut into small pieces when the mixture is set.

White Nougat Variations

This section is, again, dedicated to variations of the classic white nougat recipes including recipes for different base nuts and sometimes no nuts at all. Nougat is a wonderfully diverse confection, and once you've mastered the basics you can get creative and add a wide range of your favourite nuts and fruit.

Walnut Nougat

Walnuts work brilliantly in nougat. This recipe is unusual in that it uses gelatine. The use of gelatine in this recipe works to give your nougat a wonderful soft and chewy texture. The egg white in this recipe is also key to creating just the right consistency to your nougat, but interestingly requires no whisking.

Walnut Nougat

½ lb sugar
1 cup water
1 oz powdered gelatine
1 tsp glucose
¼ lb chopped walnuts
white of egg
1 tsp almond extract
1 tsp vanilla extract
½ tbsp icing sugar
½ tbsp corn flour

1. In a heavy-bottomed saucepan, heat the water, gelatine and sugar over a moderate heat, stirring constantly. **2.** Add the glucose and boil for eight minutes, stirring all the while. **3.** Remove the pan from the heat, allow to cool slightly, then add the egg white, the extracts and the chopped walnuts. **4.** Carefully pour the mixture onto a marble slab or lightly oiled board, and work the mixture by repeatedly folding the edges into the centre, until the ingredients are well-blended. **5.** Butter and dust a baking tin with the icing sugar and corn flour and carefully press the mixture in. **6.** Leave to set for 24 hours, and cut into squares when hard.

Soft Cherry Nougat

Fruit works brilliantly in nougat, and before the days of modern preserving techniques would have been a nifty way of preserving fruit and their precious peels. This wonderful recipe is for cherry nougat, which has an especially soft texture due to the absence of nuts. This recipe uses glace cherries, but would work just as well with any other candied fruit you have in your larder.

Soft Cherry Nougat

3/4 lb or granulated sugar
2 tsp honey or golden syrup
½ cup water
3-4 oz glace cherries, chopped
1-2 drops lemon essence
2 egg whites

1. In a heavy-bottomed saucepan, dissolve the sugar and the water over a low heat. **2.** Add the syrup or honey, and heat the mixture until it reaches 245°F, or until the mixture forms flexible strands when tested in cold water. **3.** Beat the egg whites in a large bowl, and when they form stiff peaks, gradually add the mixture from the saucepan to them, stirring all the while. **4.** Add the essence and cherries and beat until the mixture thickens. **5.** Carefully pour the mixture onto a marble slab or lightly oiled board, and work the mixture by repeatedly folding the edges into the centre until the mixture begins to hold its shape. **6.** Carefully press the mixture into oiled tins and leave overnight to set.

Rum and Raisin Nougat

It is possible to add a splash of your favourite liqueur to your nougat mixture, making this delicious confection a truly indulgent treat. Liqueurs like Khalua, Grand Marnier or Cointreau work particularly well, but this recipe uses rum as the perfect accompaniment to the sweet and chewy raisins in the nougat.

Rum and Raisin Nougat

4½ oz blanched almonds
2 oz raisins
7 oz granulated sugar
7 oz unsalted butter
3½ oz unsweetened cocoa powder
1 egg
1 egg yolk
3 tbsp rum

1. Spread the almonds on a baking tray and bake for 7-10 minutes, or until they turn golden-brown. Grind them coarsely in a pestle and mortar, being careful to stop when they resemble grains of rice. **2.** Cream together the butter and sugar in a bowl until light and fluffy. **3.** Sieve the cocoa and add it to the butter and sugar. **4.** Lightly beat together the whole egg and the egg yolk and then add the eggs to the mixture. Stir well until everything is well blended together.
5. Add the ground almonds and the liqueur. Mix thoroughly. **6.** Carefully spoon the mixture into an oiled tin. Place a chopping board or weight on top to weigh the mixture down. **7.** Turn out of the tray and and cut into small pieces to serve.

Maple Nougat

Most nougat recipes use basic granulated sugar, but their are other variations of the sweet with slightly different recipes. Maple sugar is made from the sap of sugar-maple trees and is a traditional sweetener in America and Canada. It is almost twice as sweet as regular cane sugar, making it a fantastic addition to many nougat recipes. This recipe uses the sugar, which will subtly flavour your sweets with the unmistakable taste of maple.

Maple Nougat

¾ lb maple sugar
½ cup water
2 whites of eggs
2 oz shredded almonds
1 oz chopped walnuts
1 tsp vanilla essence or orange-flower water

1. In a heavy-bottomed saucepan, dissolve the maple sugar and the water over a low heat. **2.** Heat the mixture until it reaches 239°F, or until the mixture forms flexible strands when tested in cold water. **3.** Beat the egg whites in a large bowl until form stiff peaks. **4.** Add the mixture from the saucepan, to the egg whites, stirring all the while. **5.** Add the vanilla essence and beat until the mixture thickens. **6.** Carefully pour the mixture onto a marble slab or lightly oiled board, and work the mixture by repeatedly folding the edges into the centre until it begins to hold its shape. **7.** Carefully press the mixture into oiled tins and leave overnight to set.

Chocolate Cream Nougat

Adding chocolate to your nougat is a perfect way to make an extra-special batch of nougat. The hint of chocolate and generous helping of nuts will give this nougat a wonderfully rich taste and texture.

Chocolate Cream Nougat

1 lb granulated sugar
1 cup water
1 tsp glucose
1 oz butter
1 tsp vanilla essence
¼ lb shredded almonds
2-3 oz chocolate (unsweetened)
2 tsp cream

1. In a heavy-bottomed saucepan, dissolve the sugar in the water, stirring over a low heat. **2.** Add the glucose and butter and boil until 239 F, or until the mixture forms flexible strands when tested in cold water. **3.** In a separate pan, begin melting the chocolate in a bowl over simmering water. **4.** Remove the pan containing the nougat mixture from the heat and allow the bubbles to subside. Carefully pour the mixture onto a lightly oiled board or marble slab. **5.** Pour the melted chocolate onto the nougat mixture, and work it in by folding the edges into the centre. Repeat until the chocolate is blended, and then return the mixture to the pan and add the cream and vanilla essence. **6.** Stir the mixture well until it is blended, and thin enough to pour. Add the chopped nuts, then carefully pour into an oiled tin. **7.** Leave to set overnight.

Wartime Recipes

This next selection of recipes would have been useful recipes to master during wartime rationing in Britain, when sugar was scarce. It was commonplace for fruits and vegetables and other natural sources of sugar to be used to make sweets at the start of the 20th century, and this method of cooking really took off during the war. Using the natural sugars in fruits and syrups can make it possible to create an array of delicious sweets, with much less sugar needed than for classic recipes.

Wartime Recipes

The last recipe of the book includes the rather unusual addition of tomato. This recipe for tomato nougatine was first found in the 1912 book, 'Candy-Making Revolutionized', and uses the distinctive flavour of ginger to give the finished sweets a subtly spicy sweetness.

Wartime Recipes

2 cups sugar
⅔ cup corn syrup
⅓ cup clear honey
⅓ cup strained, cooked tomato
3 egg whites
½ cup almonds
½ cup crystallised ginger, chopped finely

1. Beat the egg whites in a large bowl until they form stiff peaks. **2.** In a heavy-bottomed saucepan, heat the sugar, corn syrup, honey and tomato until the mixture reaches 260°F, or until the mixture forms a hard ball when tested in cold water. **3.** Remove the pan from the heat, and start gradually adding half a cup of the sugar syrup to the beaten egg whites. **4.** Return the remaining sugar syrup to the heat and cook until it reaches 290°F, or until the mixture forms firm strands when tested in cold water. **5.** Remove the mixture from the heat and add it to the egg whites, beating continuously. **6.** Add to this the almonds and ginger, and carefully pour the mixture into a buttered tin. **7.** You can add a layer of rice paper to the top of the nougat before it cools, or simply mark it into squares.

Pecan Patties

This rather nifty little recipe for pecan patties is unusual in that it uses no sugar at all. A generous measure of maple syrup in this recipe provides all the sweetness needed, and the distinctive flavour works wonderfully with the crunch of the pecan nuts.

Pecan Patties

5 cups maple syrup
1/4 lb butter
1 1/2 cups pecan nuts, chopped

1. In a heavy-bottomed saucepan, heat the syrup and the butter until the mixture reaches 240°F, or until the mixture forms a soft ball when tested in cold water. **2.** Remove the pan from the heat, and stir in the pecan nuts. **3.** Carefully pour the mixture into an oiled tin, and mark into squares when cool.

The Etiquette of Serving

The Etiquette of Serving

Finding new and interesting recipes to impress dinner party guests could be a daunting prospect for a hostess, but offering carefully crafted homemade nougat to guests at the end of the evening was seen to be an elegant touch.

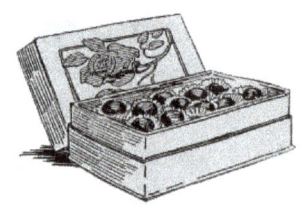

The Etiquette of Serving

Traditionally, nougat would have been served at the end of supper, perhaps to accompany coffee. A selection of nougat was placed in a pretty dish and offered to guests. A classic recipe nougat made a very dainty alternative to dessert after a heavy meal.

The Etiquette of Serving

Today, you can still find beautiful antique glass and china dishes specifically for serving sweets. Some have lids but some are made without lids and are perfect for serving your nougat to guests at the dinner table. Glass dishes are perfect for displaying your hard work, and you can add a linen napkin or paper doily to your dish before filling with nougat if you prefer.

Gifts

There is nothing nicer than a handmade gift, and what better way to make the most of your new-found nougat-making skills than to give it to a loved one as a present. Homemade nougat makes the perfect Christmas or birthday gift, and you can even add your loved ones' favourite ingredients to the recipe for a truly personal touch.

Gifts

Fold your nougat into rice paper to make sure it doesn't stick together and carefully wrap your gift. Small cardboard boxes from craft shops are also perfect this, and can be wrapped in festive paper, too.

We hope you have enjoyed this little book about the wonderful world of making nougat. We hope we have we have been able to provide a wealth of useful and practical information that can be passed on again, so that these invaluable skills will not be lost.

Credits and Attributions

Cover Image, Title page and Page 4 - This work is a derivative of "1956-Electrolux" is copyright © October 17, 2009 James Vaughn, x-ray delta one, made available on Flickr under Creative Commons Attribution 2.0 Generic (CC BY 2.0) http://www.flickr.com/photos/x-ray_delta_one/4017899831/sizes/l/in/faves-90808113@N04/

Page 10 - This work is a derivative of "It's All You Need" is Copyright © 1950 Posted by noluck_boston, made available on vintage-ads.livejournal.com http://vintage-ads.livejournal.com/tag/cleaning

Page 13 - This work is a derivative of "Waste Not want not" is Copyright © 1914 Canadian Food Board, Hamilton [Ontario, Canada] : Howell Lith., made available on www.loc.gov/ under The Public Domain Licence http://www.loc.gov/pictures/item/2005696499/

Page 21 - This work is a derivative of "Do with less, so they'll have enough! Rationing gives you your fair share" is Copyright © 1943, posted by United States. Office of War Information. Division of Public Inquiries, made available on UNT Digital Library under The Public Domain Licence http://digital.library.unt.edu/ark:/67531/metadc538/?q=Rationing

Page 22 - This work is a derivative of "Your Sugar Ration 1917 - ca. 1919" is Copyright ©1917 U.S. Food Administration. Educational Division. Advertising Section, made available on Wikimedia under The Public Domain Licence http://commons.wikimedia.org/wiki/File:%22This_Store_is_pledged_to_conform_to_the_Sugar_Regulations_of_the_Food_Administration._Your_Sugar_Ration_is_2lbs._per_mo_-_NARA_-_512525.jpg

Page 26 - This work is a derivative of "Narragansett Electric Co.'s Fat and Grease – Pass the Ammunition (1943)" is Copyright © 1943 posted by Ginevra, midniterose, made available on vintage-ads.livejournal.com http://vintage-ads.livejournal.com/tag/ww2%20rationing

Page 28 - This work is a derivative of "Pg. 94, COPPER CANDY LADLE. Fig 7" is Copyright © 1896, The Candy Maker's Guide, by Fletcher Manufacturing Company made available on Gutenburg under The Public Domain Licence http://www.gutenberg.org/files/30293/30293-h/30293-h.htm

Page 29 - This work is a derivative of "Pg. 94, COPPER CANDY LADLE. Fig 8" is Copyright © 1896, The Candy Maker's Guide, by Fletcher Manufacturing Company made available on Gutenburg under The Public Domain Licence http://www.gutenberg.org/files/30293/30293-h/30293-h.htm

Page 30 Page 31 Page 32 Page 34 - This work is a derivative of "whenmotherletsus pg 17" is Copyright © 1915 New York, Moffat, Yard and company, made available on Archive under The Public Domain Licence http://archive.org/details/whenmotherletsus00bach

Page 32 - This work is a derivative of "LIFE Dec 12, 1955 hamilton watches christmas spread" is Copyright © 1955, posted by Jocelmeow, made available on vintage-ads.livejournal.com http://vintage-ads.livejournal.com/tag/1945

Page 35 - This work is a derivative of "Maxwell House Coffee (1950) " is Copyright © 1950 posted by, pikkewyntjie made available on vintage-ads.livejournal.com http://vintage-ads.livejournal.com/tag/1950

Page 39 - This work is a derivative of "whenmotherletsus pg 18" is Copyright © 1915 New York, Moffat, Yard and company, made available on Archive under The Public Domain Licence http://archive.org/details/whenmotherletsus00bach

Page 41 - This work is a derivative of "Diced Cream of America Co., 1949" is Copyright © 1949, posted by Man Writing Slash (write_light), made available on vintage-ads.livejournal.com http://vintage-ads.livejournal.com/tag/1949

Page 88 - This work is a derivative of "whenmotherletsus pg 26" is Copyright © 1915 New York, Moffat, Yard and company, made available on Archive under The Public Domain Licence http://archive.org/details/whenmotherletsus00bach

Page 89 - This work is a derivative of "Vintage ChinaTaken from Mrs Beetons Everyday Cookery & Housekeeping" is Copyright © 1893, posted by tiffany terry, libertygrace0 made available on flickr under Creative commons Attribution 2.0 Generic (CC BY 2.0) http://www.flickr.com/photos/35168673@N03/4392797084/in/set-72157627296287304

Page 90 - This work is a derivative of "Three legged glass dish" is Copyright © January 27, 2012 , Joanna Bourne, made available on flickr under Creative commons Attribution 2.0 Generic (CC BY 2.0) http://www.flickr.com/photos/66992990@N00/6773469145/sizes/l/

Page 92 - This work is a derivative of "Tiffany Blue" is Copyright © May 18, 2008, Jill Clardy, made available on flickr under Creative commons Attribution 2.0 Generic (CC BY 2.0) http://www.flickr.com/photos/jillclardy/2523850043/

Page 93 - This work is a derivative of "UH-OH - Oreo / Nabisco, 1951" is Copyright © 1951, posted by Man Writing Slash (write_light), made available on vintage-ads.livejournal.com http://vintage-ads.livejournal.com/tag/1919

www.ingramcontent.com/pod-product-compliance
Lightning Source LLC
Chambersburg PA
CBHW050114170426
43198CB00014B/2570